Keep this pocket-sized Frith book with you when you are travelling around London.

Whether you are in your car or on foot, you will enjoy an evocative journey back in time. Compare the London of old with what you can see today —enjoy fascinating vistas along the River Thames in its heyday as a port; tour the famous sights and beauty spots, including the Tower of London and Trafalgar Square; promenade in London's great parks with the fashionable rich; wander the streets and alleyways, from Oxford Street and the West End through to the bustling, commercial City. See the many alterations to London that have taken place during our lives, and which we may have taken for granted.

At the turn of a page you will gain fascinating insights into London's unique history.

FRANCIS FRITH's
pocket ALBUM

LONDON

A POCKET ALBUM

Adapted from an original book by
TERENCE SACKETT

First published in the United Kingdom in 2004 by
Frith Book Company Ltd

ISBN 1-85937-869-2

Text and Design copyright © Frith Book Company Ltd
Photographs copyright © The Francis Frith Collection

The Frith photographs and the Frith logo are reproduced under licence from Heritage
Photographic Resources Ltd, the owners of the Frith archive and trademarks

British Library Cataloguing in Publication Data

London—A Pocket Album
Adapted from an original book by Terence Sackett

Frith Book Company Ltd
Frith's Barn, Teffont,
Salisbury, Wiltshire SP3 5QP
Tel: +44 (0) 1722 716 376
Email: info@francisfrith.co.uk
www.francisfrith.co.uk

Printed and bound in Great Britain by MPG, Bodmin

Front Cover: THREADNEEDLE STREET AND THE ROYAL EXCHANGE
c1910 L130193

The colour-tinting is for illustrative purposes only, and is not intended to be historically accurate.

Frontispiece: EROS AND PICCADILLY CIRCUS 1887 L130186

CONTENTS

FRANCIS FRITH
VICTORIAN PIONEER

*Francis Frith, founder of the world-famous photographical
archive, was a complex and multi-talented man. A devout
Quaker and a highly successful Victorian businessman, he was philosophic
by nature and pioneering in outlook. By 1855 he had already established a
wholesale grocery business in Liverpool, and sold it for the astonishing sum
of £200,000, which is the equivalent today of over £15,000,000. Now in
his thirties, and captivated by the new science of photography, Frith set out
on a series of pioneering journeys up the Nile and to the Near East.*

INTRIGUE AND EXPLORATION

He was the first photographer to venture beyond the sixth cataract of the
Nile. Africa was still the mysterious 'Dark Continent', and Stanley and
Livingstone's historic meeting was a decade into the future. The conditions
for picture taking confound belief. He laboured for hours in his wicker dark-
room in the sweltering heat of the desert, while the volatile chemicals fizzed
dangerously in their trays. Back in London he exhibited his photographs and
was 'rapturously cheered' by members of the Royal Society. His reputation as
a photographer was made overnight.

VENTURE OF A LIFE-TIME

By the 1870s the railways had threaded their way across the country, and
Bank Holidays and half-day Saturdays had been made obligatory by Act of
Parliament. All of a sudden the working man and his family were able to
enjoy days out, take holidays, and see a little more of the world.

With typical business acumen, Francis Frith foresaw that these new
tourists would enjoy having souvenirs to commemorate their days out. For

4

the next thirty years he travelled the country by train and by pony and trap, producing fine photographs of seaside resorts and beauty spots that were keenly bought by millions of Victorians. These prints were painstakingly pasted into family albums and pored over during the dark nights of winter, rekindling precious memories of summer excursions. Frith's studio was soon supplying retail shops all over the country, and by 1890 F Frith & Co had become the greatest specialist photographic publishing company in the world, with over 2,000 sales outlets, and pioneered the picture postcard.

FRANCIS FRITH'S LEGACY

Francis Frith had died in 1898 at his villa in Cannes, his great project still growing. The archive he created continued in business for another seventy years. By 1970 it contained over a third of a million pictures showing 7,000 British towns and villages.

Frith's legacy to us today is of immense significance and value, for the magnificent archive of evocative photographs he created provides a unique record of change in the cities, towns and villages throughout Britain over a century and more. Frith and his fellow studio photographers revisited locations many times down the years to update their views, compiling for us an enthralling and colourful pageant of British life and character.

We are fortunate that Frith was dedicated to recording the minutiae of everyday life. For it is this sheer wealth of visual data, the painstaking chronicle of changes in dress, transport, street layouts, buildings, housing, engineering and landscape that captivates us so much today, offering us a powerful link with the past and with the lives of our ancestors.

Computers have now made it possible for Frith's many thousands of images to be accessed almost instantly. The archive offers every one of us an opportunity to examine the places where we and our families have lived and worked down the years. Its images, depicting our shared past, are now bringing pleasure and enlightenment to millions around the world a century and more after his death.

LONDON

AN INTRODUCTION

Until the end of the 18th century London was a compact city. Its merchants lived in the square mile and the aristocracy in the more fashionable areas of Piccadilly and the West End.

Beyond Park Lane, however, there was a wilderness of forest and mire, where footpads and highwayman lurked. Londoners were regularly accosted in the Strand. Many preferred to travel by water on the River Thames.

In the Victorian era the city grew at an extraordinary rate as the Empire spread and wealth returned to the coffers of the London banks. Whole neighbourhoods of ramshackle housing were demolished and the great thoroughfares we know today were created. Nash remodelled much of the West End, and great houses and mansions lined the leafy thoroughfares that were once grazing land for the city's flocks of sheep. Public spaces such as Trafalgar Square and Piccadilly Circus were created and richly embellished by public sculpture and memorials commemorating Britain's historic past.

The 1851 Great Exhibition symbolised the country's new wealth and prestige. The great glass halls conceived by Paxton were filled to bursting with triumphs of industry and engineering endeavour, and the world flocked to enjoy a glimpse of the exciting future.

The City of London developed gradually into the centre of world finance. London's burgeoning banks and insurance companies clamoured for space in the overcrowded square mile. Further widespread demolition followed, and new streets of Victorian Gothic offices were constructed, heavy and sepulchral in character. Here many thousands of clerks and office workers laboured day in and day out. Traffic congested the newly built or refurbished roads and bridges and Londoners struggled with the complexities of city life very much as we do today.

The poor were ever present. Thousands of country people flocked to London with the promise of work. Yet with increasing mechanisation of production traditional crafts and trades were swiftly superseded, throwing thousands into the streets to earn a few shillings. London's street traders were a legend, their guile and cunning offering them the only hope of survival in a hostile city.

For centuries London's wealth had been fuelled by river traffic. Great ships plied the estuary of the Thames to unload at the many new docks that were constructed as far upriver as London Bridge. The wharves and quays resounded with the cries of stevedores and dock workers unloading coal, timber and the raw materials of engineering. There were also exotic imports from China and Asia to tempt the wealthy.

By the time of Queen Victoria's Jubilee in 1897 the face of the capital would have been almost unrecognisable to an eighteenth century Londoner. The streets and buildings stretched out into the countryside and millions of people had moved out of the expensive centre to newly-built suburbs to become commuters. The rate of change had been bewildering and relentless. Everyone was touched by it and many suffered as a result of it. Yet there was no going back. London's expansion has never slowed since. With its beautiful streets and buildings, and its unique position as financial centre of Europe and the colonies, it had justly earned its reputation as the greatest city in the world.

LONDON, ROYAL EXCHANGE 1886 L130012

A carriage with top-hatted coachman waits patiently outside
one of Cheyne Walk's many grand Georgian brick houses.
Graceful plane trees screen residents from the more
boisterous life on the water. A fleet of barges, their sales
furled, are berthed at the quay.

CHEYNE WALK
CHELSEA 1890 L130087

This tranquil street of handsome houses fringing the river was built in 1708. Chelsea had long been the haunt of artists and writers - Thomas Carlyle lived at 5, Cheyne Walk for almost half a century. Other illustrious residents, including Philip Wilson Steer, Whistler and Rossetti, were his close neighbours. Boats squat in the mud under the embankment.

CHEYNE WALK, CHELSEA
1890 L130084

Until 1878 all but three of the bridges over
the Thames were owned by private companies
who levelled tolls on foot passengers. In 1879
this beautiful bridge of three airy spans,
topped with decorative towers, was made free
for public access.

ALBERT BRIDGE
c1900 L130129

CHELSEA EMBANKMENT
1890 L130083

This Lambeth river frontage presents a very different face to the more refined Chelsea scene across the river. Here is a clutter of ramshackle warehouses, timber-yards and wharves. The flimsy houses were clearly not designed to face the water, for the windows are few and diminutive. The crumbling facades bring a clear impression of neglect and poverty.

LAMBETH RIVERSIDE
1880 L130120

A steamer, with a party of sightseers on board, has just left the quay heading down river. The women cluster at the stern under parasols. A little further along on the left is Cleopatra's Needle. This far-famed monument was transported to Britain through the treacherous Bay of Biscay from the deserts of Egypt, where it had lain buried and forgotten in the sands. It took considerable ingenuity to erect it in such a close space, for it is almost seventy feet in height.

VICTORIA EMBANKMENT
1890 L130189

This fine bridge is one of the most dazzling structures spanning London's river and was constructed in 1862 at the cost of £250,000. With the waters at low tide as they are here, critics have suggested the bridge has an ungraceful 'lanky' appearance. Its uniquely light construction was the cause of trepidation amongst Londoners, for passengers on horse drawn buses felt an unnerving vibration under the wheels as they passed over.

WESTMINSTER BRIDGE
C1900 L130303

Gulls forage for food in the frozen wastes. The ice has broken and the waters of the river released. Canova considered the old Waterloo Bridge, with its nine elliptical arches, to be one of the most magnificent in Europe. Originally called Strand Bridge, it was opened in 1817 on the anniversary of the Battle of Waterloo.

OLD WATERLOO BRIDGE
1895 L130052

*This panorama of the river through broad
lawns and lofty trees reveals the bridge's
graceful character. Engineered by John Rennie,
it was well over 1,000 feet long and
surmounted by an open balustrade. In 1924,
after engineering reports of a dangerous
weakening of one of the main arches, the old
bridge was closed to traffic. Work on the new
Waterloo Bridge was started in 1937.*

OLD WATERLOO BRIDGE
1902 L130155

This famous vista, taken from Bankside, shows the glorious dome of St Paul's rising over the roofs of London. The river is edged not with the anonymous and monumental office blocks we see today but with a pleasing clutter of wharves and warehouses. The river was a populous place of work where barges and a thousand other vessels plied. On the right is the colliery wharf of the Weardale Iron and Coal Company.

WATERFRONT BY ST PAUL'S
1890 L130017

The delightful Temple Gardens once extended right the way down to the river. Here were clipped green lawns and exquisite quadrangles. The fortunate few could enjoy a few precious moments away from the bustle of the city streets above. The imposing arch is in the monumental Egyptian style. In the background is Waterloo Bridge.

EMBANKMENT FROM
TEMPLE PIER 1890 L130077

The halfpenny toll on the original Blackfriars Bridge caused riots, and in 1780 angry protesters burned down the toll-house. After a succession of expensive repairs a replacement was suggested, and the present bridge was erected in 1864 at a cost of £265,000. With its colossal piers, and recesses set on pillars of polished Aberdeen granite, Blackfriars Bridge has been censured by critics for being 'gaudy'.

BLACKFRIARS BRIDGE
1890 L130070

So busy was London bridge at peak times that the authorities were compelled to station police constables along the central rib of the roadway to encourage a smooth flow of traffic. All vehicles moving at walking pace were ushered abruptly to the kerb sides so that swifter carriages could enjoy a clear passage.

LONDON BRIDGE
C1890 L130178

This five-arched granite structure was constructed in 1827 from the designs of John Rennie. Its excessive cost was once the talk of the city. Estimates ran as high as two and a half million pounds. In 1869 it was faced with cubes of Aberdeen granite. In the background is the imposing column of the Monument.

LONDON BRIDGE
c1900 L130317

LONDON BRIDGE
1890 L130034

The traffic jam is clearly not a modern phenomenon. London Bridge is thronged with cabs, carriers, brewers' drays, hay wagons, omnibuses and carriages. A dense procession of top-hatted gentlemen hurry along the pavement to their city offices. London Bridge's lamp-posts were cast from the metal of French cannons captured in the Peninsula War.

OPENING OF TOWER BRIDGE

1894 L130019

The raised footway at the top of the towers, 140 feet above the level of the river, was closed in 1909 after a spate of suicides. In the foreground lies the Pool of London, the province of London watermen for generations. The river, at the end of Victoria's reign, is still busy with flat barges and sailing ships. In the background are the pinnacles of the Tower of London.

TOWER BRIDGE
1896 L130519

Uniquely for London bridges, the bascules of Tower Bridge can be raised or lowered to permit the passage of high-peaked vessels. Driven by steam, the hydraulic machinery hoisted the heavy 1,000 ton bascules to their raised positions in two minutes.

TOWER BRIDGE OPENING
c1895 L130061

Where London's other bridges are dignified and utilitarian, Tower Bridge, with its 'daring majesty' cocks a snook at Victorian formality. Barry permitted Sir Horace Jones to encase his steel skeleton in stone until it resembled an iced cake. Mock Gothic turrets were added, a profusion of sharply arched windows and much other sham detailing. To many the stupendous structure had the look of an ornate medieval castle.

TOWER BRIDGE
1910 L130058

It is dawn and stevedores, carpenters, coopers and ropemakers are arriving by boat to begin the day's toil. They clamber eagerly up the rickety steps to stake their claim to work - most were poorly-paid casual workers hired daily. The thicket of wooden scaffolds would give a modern-day health and safety inspector a heart attack.

THAMES SHIPBUILDING
c1910 L130056

The cityside banks of the Thames were busy with stevedores and dockers during the Victorian era, for London's river had been the source of its prosperity for centuries. However, by 1910 the industry was parlously overmanned, and the docks had gone into sharp decline.

OLD FERRY WHARF
c1890 L130085

Away from the boisterous life of the river, Cheyne Walk, with its narrow, balconied houses and modish shops, was a haven of gentility, dedicated to refined if somewhat Bohemian pursuits. In the background is Chelsea Old Church, which suffered extensive bomb damage in the War.

CHEYNE WALK
OLD CHURCH 1890 L130086

WATERMAN'S ARMS,

CHELSEA 1875 L130123

Hyde Park has been called London's park 'par excellence'. Rotten Row, a corruption of route du roi, was a ride set aside for equestrians and fashionable promenaders. During afternoons in the London season, it was densely thronged with carriages parading their smart passengers around at little more than walking pace. The inevitable more refined traffic jams ended in polite deadlock.

ROTTEN ROW
1890 L130171

*Park Lane, once the desolate by-road known as Tiburn
Lane, was a refined street of palatial mansions enjoying
expansive vistas of the Park. These great houses included
Grosvenor House, the home of the Marquess of Westminster,
Holdernesse House, the residence of the Marquess of
Londonderry, and Dorchester House.*

PARK LANE
1890 L130166

Hyde Park extends from Piccadilly westwards to Kensington Gardens. Its 360-acres of open green space were called by William Pitt 'the lung of London'. 'Here', writes Thomas Miller, 'the pride and beauty of England may be seen upon their own stage; and on a fine day in the season no other spot in the world can outrival in rich display and chaste grandeur the scene which is here presented'.

HYDE PARK
1890 L130105

This graceful ornamental fountain was erected in 1875 at the southern end of Park Lane at the junction with Hamilton Place. Designed by Sir Hamo Thornycroft, it incorporates three heroic-size marble figures of Shakespeare, Milton and Chaucer. The statue is surmounted by the gilded bronze winged figure of Fame, poised with one foot on a globe.

PARK LANE

1900 L130035

The arch of this impressive monument was originally crowned by Wyatt's colossal equestrian statue of the England's military darling, the Iron Duke. In the 1880s, when the French wars were long forgotten, it was moved to Aldershot and replaced by the dramatic bronze by Adrian Jones, an allegorical rendering of Peace dropping out of the heavens onto the chariot of war.

THE WELLINGTON ARCH,
HYDE PARK CORNER
1915 L130202

Decimus Burton's impressive arch is topped by a decorative frieze depicting horsemen, the design imitated from the Elgin Marbles which were on display in the British Museum. So much of this luxurious neighbourhood mimics the glories of classical Greece.

HYDE PARK CORNER
1900 L130003

Only a century and a half ago Hyde Park was bordered by mire and wilderness. Londoners tended market gardens close by which are now smothered by the buildings of Kensington. In the 18th century it was considered foolhardy to venture here after dark. Travellers joined forces to ward off the attentions of highwaymen.

HYDE PARK CORNER
C1900 L130169

The handsome triple-arched gateway, with its classical screen and groups of Ionic columns, was intended originally to create a noble approach to the Park from Buckingham Palace. It was designed and built in 1828 by Decimus Burton. The omnibus on the right, heading for Pimlico, is advertising the famous furnishing and decorating emporium of Maples.

HYDE PARK CORNER
c1908 L130151

To the right of the arch is Apsley House, one of only two or three of Piccadilly's great houses to survive. Known popularly as 'Number One, London', it was built by Robert Adam in the 1770s. It was bought by the Duke of Wellington in 1817 and here were held glittering banquets celebrating the victory at Waterloo until his death in 1852.

APSLEY HOUSE,
HYDE PARK CORNER
C1920 L130238

In the time of James I the leafy grounds where this celebrated royal palace now stands grew mulberry bushes for the silk industry. The palace was built in its original form in the early 1700s and adapted to the Palladian style by John Nash in the 1830s. The Lord Chamberlain was always inundated with requests to view from the public, but permits were only granted to view the royal stables.

BUCKINGHAM PALACE
C1890 L130173

Marble Arch stood here in the Mall until 1850, when it was removed to its present position at the top of Park Lane. The Mall, an expansive and formal approach to the Palace, is fringed with limes, planes and elms, and skirts the north side of the diminutive St James's Park. Here, in freezing winters, Londoners enjoyed skating on the pond.

BUCKINGHAM PALACE
AND THE MALL C1955 L1305050

EROS AND PICCADILLY CIRCUS

1887 L130186

This famous junction was once known as Regent Circus and developed out of Nash's elegant modelling of Regent Street. George IV likened Piccadilly Circus to an illusion of preventing 'the sensation of crossing Piccadilly being perceived'. In 1886 many of its buildings were demolished and the open space considerably enlarged.

PICCADILLY CIRCUS
1890 L130002

Conceived and built by John Nash in 1813, this famous thoroughfare has been said to represent 'the highest beauty of street architecture.' The bold, sweeping curve of the Quadrant originally incorporated an open Doric arcade of 270 columns supporting a balustraded roof. However, the heavy cast shadows attracted 'undesirable company' and the arcade was eventually removed in 1848.

REGENT STREET

AND THE QUADRANT 1900 L130163

This view looks north towards Oxford Street. Nash's handsome terraces were spurned by London's affluent classes, for stucco was considered common. Some said that his glorious creation was compromised by poor building work, but all agreed that Nash conjured for this region of the West End a genteel and polished atmosphere that has considerably added to its prosperity down the years.

REGENT STREET
c1890 L130079

The paintings that formed the basis of Britain's national collection were purchased for £57,000 in 1824 from J Angerstein. The exhibition halls created on the north side of Trafalgar Square to display the lavish canvases were not universally admired. One Victorian critic believed 'the authorities showed a frugal mind in the low elevation of the building with its pepper-box turrets and insignificant dome'.

THE NATIONAL GALLERY
FROM DUNCANNON STREET 1897 L130054

This exquisite Royal church was designed and erected by the architect James Gibbs in the 1720s. The expansive portico is generally admired, but the heavy steeple is said to lack elegance. Nell Gwynne was buried here.

ST MARTIN-IN-THE-FIELDS
CHURCH, TRAFALGAR SQUARE 1890 L130133

This is arguably the most famous public open space in the world. Sir Robert Peel called it 'one of the finest sites in Europe'. It was created in the 1830s on the site of the King's Mews and a jumble of decrepit buildings known popularly as Bermuda, Caribee, and Porridge Islands, where the poor of London frequented a plethora of cheap cook-shops.

TRAFALGAR SQUARE
1890 L130190

Nelson's column was not the first choice of monument to embellish Trafalgar Square - a Colonel Trench had proposed a great pyramid to dwarf St Paul's. Of Portland stone, and 145 feet high, it was erected in 1843. The figure of Nelson was carved from three massive stones, the largest of which weighed thirty tons.

TRAFALGAR SQUARE
1890 L130161

Four immense bronze lions by Landseer guard the foot of the memorial. The fountains, conceived by Sir Charles Barry, were considered by some Victorians to detract from the overall magnificence of the monument, 'because of the ridiculous insufficiency of their jets of water'.

TRAFALGAR SQUARE
1900 L130062

ST GILES
1885 L130215

A bustling street scene at the junction of Oxford Street and the Charing Cross Road. We think of advertising as a modern phenomenon. Yet the Victorian businessman was never slow nor discreet in proclaiming his sales message. These omnibuses are smothered in posters for legendary brands - Dewar's Whisky, Schweppes, Pears Soap, and Swan Vestas.

ST GILES CIRCUS
1910 L130218

WESTMINSTER ABBEY

c1867 L130142

This sublime abbey, scene of many coronations down the centuries, is probably the most famous of English religious buildings, and considered the pinnacle of European Gothic architecture. Henry II began the reshaping of Edward the Confessor's old church. Restyling continued until well into the 16th century. The abbey was embellished by its lofty twin towers in the early 1700s.

WESTMINSTER ABBEY
1908 L130150

This 'superb temple of legislation' in Tudor Gothic was built to replace the old medieval Palace which burned down in 1834. Covering nearly eight acres of ground, it was constructed to Sir Charles Barry's design, although its intricate ornament and detailing were conceived and wrought by that master of Victorian Gothic, Augustus Pugin.

HOUSES OF PARLIAMENT
1886 L130188

The finest prospect of Barry's Palace of Westminster is to be
enjoyed from the river, where the facade extends to a length
of almost a thousand feet. The strong vertical detailing was
clearly intended to create the impression of a just and God-
fearing Parliament aspiring to the Heavenly virtues.

HOUSES OF PARLIAMENT
1908 L130149

PARLIAMENT SQUARE
1890 L130008

In 1848 a serious drainage problem was discovered inside the Parliament building. A main sewer, passing directly underneath, was discharging into the river under Westminster Bridge. The malodorous gas from this sewer was so dreadful that it extinguished the lamps of the investigating party. Many of the underground apartments were found to be little more than open cesspools.

HOUSES OF PARLIAMENT
1890 L130162

On the south bank of the Thames, opposite the Palace of Westminster is this handsome building, for centuries the official residence of the Archbishops of Canterbury. The entrance is through a Gothic gateway, the ground floor of which was once a prison. The Lollard's Tower adjoins the west end of the chapel. Here the Lollards, followers of Wycliffe, were imprisoned and tortured.

LAMBETH PALACE
c1965 L1305068

This colossal building, once home of the controversial Greater London Council, was designed by Ralph Knott and begun in 1912. Though it sits heavily on the Embankment, its broad facades and massed arches in the Piranesi style bring it a monumental dignity.'

COUNTY HALL
C1955 L1305043

The cries of traders echo through the expansive square, planned by Inigo Jones. The scene has been described by a contemporary guidebook: 'All night long the rumble of heavy wagons seldom ceases, and before daylight the market is crowded. The very loading of these wagons is a wonder, and the wall-like regularity with which cabbages, cauliflowers and turnips are built up to a height of some twelve feet is nothing short of a miracle'.

COVENT GARDEN MARKET
1900 L130025

Serious building work is in progress in this normally sedate street. On the extreme right an area has been cordoned off with barriers, and beyond are the towers of hoists and cranes. Steam funnels into the sky from stationery engines and, in the foreground, a handcart is piled high with bricks. The rush-hour traffic presses a way through as best it can.

PARLIAMENT STREET AND WHITEHALL
1880 L130016

FLOWER SELLERS,

COVENT GARDEN 1885 L130216

FLOWER SELLERS,
COVENT GARDEN 1877 L130117

The cross that gave the area its name was destroyed in 1647. From this point all distances in London are measured. Moreover, a line drawn through it is said to separate the London of pleasure and fashion from that of work and business. The railway station occupies the ground floor of the prestigious company-owned Charing Cross Hotel.

CHARING CROSS
1890 L130180

From early morning until midnight, The Strand is London's busiest street and invariably congested with traffic. It was originally the waterside thoroughfare between the City and Westminster, and it is from this that it derives its name. In earlier days The Strand was a threatening neighbourhood, and many travellers preferred to take a boat rather than pick their way along the ill-paved street and be jostled by pickpockets.

THE STRAND
1890 L130033

The Gaiety Theatre dominates the corner where the Aldwych breaks off from the Strand. Theatre goers were enjoying performances by Jose Collins in 'Our Nell'. The glittering building was designed by the very fashionable architect Norman Shaw and opened to theatre goers in 1903. It replaced an older theatre of the same name set between Wellington Street and Catherine Street.

THE STRAND
1915 L130191

Five years on from the previous photograph, the play showing at the Gaiety Theatre is 'Love Lies' starring Stanley Lupino. The Aldwych sweeps off sharply to the north towards Kingsway, leaving an island of fine buildings between it and the Strand. The scheme for the development of the locality was completed in 1905, involving the demolition of twenty-eight acres of crooked lanes and ways.

THE ALDWYCH
c1920 L130304

This imposing, ornate gateway once stood where the Strand becomes Fleet Street, and was erected in 1672 to a design by Wren. The effigies portray Stuart monarchs. Beneath its arch Queen Victoria and Albert passed on their way to State services at St Paul's. By the 1860s it was causing considerable traffic congestion and there were heated debates in the press about its future. It was finally removed in 1878 and re-erected at Waltham Cross.

TEMPLE BAR
1875 L130141

This quaint old house sits on a corner in Lincoln's Inn Fields. It has been claimed, probably erroneously, that it is the original of 'the Old Curiosity Shop' made immortal by Dickens as the home of 'Little Nell'. In this 1950s view it has become an exclusive antique shop but in Victorian times it was a rather dingy emporium owned by H Poole, a jobbing stationer.

THE OLD CURIOSITY SHOP
C1955 L1305039

Opposite Gray's Inn Road is Staple Inn. It was once the meeting place for wool merchants with a custom house where wool dues were collected. Originally the exclusive province of lawyers, in later years many celebrated figures took rooms in the building, including Dr Johnson, who wrote 'Rasselas' here to help defray his mother's funeral expenses.

STAPLE INN
C1875 L130136

The magnificent frontage of half-timbered work is the finest in London. Here the plaster rendering shown in the previous photograph has been stripped off revealing a wealth of timbers. The shops have been considerably smartened up. New buildings flank it on both sides, that on the right housing a discount bookshop.

STAPLE INN
c1886 L130174

'The newest fashion newspaper and the oldest-style tavern still jostle each other now as they did a century or more ago.' This bustling street was once the home of the British press. The working day here ran for a full twenty-four hours, with printers and reporters crowding the bars day and night. Crowning the scene in the distance is the glorious dome of St Paul's.

FLEET STREET
1890 L130080

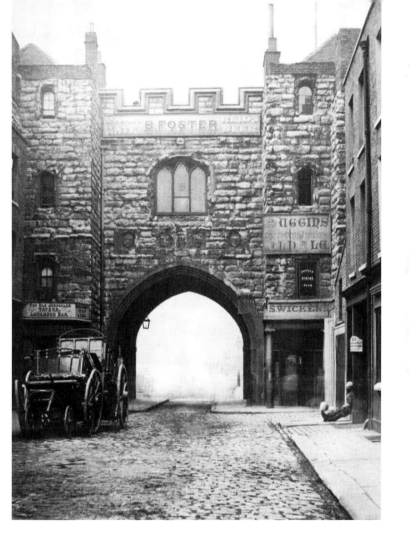

ST JOHN'S GATE,
CLERKENWELL c1870 L130144

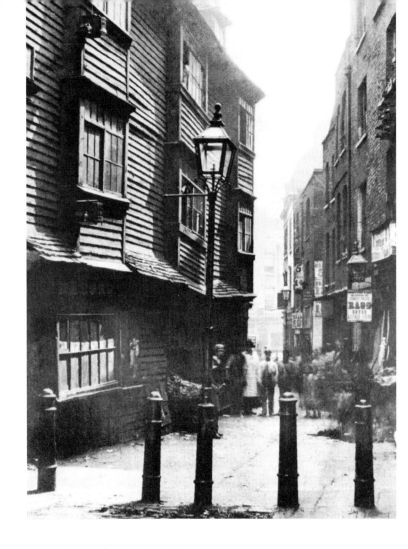

PETER'S LANE,
CLERKENWELL 1880 L130096

LUDGATE HILL
1897 L130037

The Hand-in-Hand Fire and Life Insurance Society building stands at the junction of these two streets close by Blackfriars Bridge. It was established in 1696 and by 1890 had amassed accumulated funds of over two million pounds. To its right is the railway bridge from Holborn Viaduct Station.

THE HAND-IN-HAND OFFICE

NEW BRIDGE STREET AND QUEEN VICTORIA STREET   1904 L130306

OXFORD ARMS,

WARWICK LANE c1875 L130122

This panoramic vista of the City and St Paul's was probably taken from
the southern tip of Southwark Bridge. In early days Queenhithe on the
north bank of the Thames was a significant port for the landing of fish
and corn. Its position above London Bridge - the successful docks were
all in broader reaches down-river - led to its inevitable decline.

ST PAUL'S FROM ACROSS THE RIVER 1890 L130126

Perched on the summit of Ludgate Hill at almost the highest point in the City, Wren's masterpiece is the pride of London. In the form of a cross, it is built in the Corinthian style, and surmounted by the giant dome which rises on arches over the centre. Many great men and women are buried here, including Wren himself, James Barry, Sir Joshua Reynolds, Opie and Landseer.

ST PAUL'S CATHEDRAL
1890 L130078

The heart of the Square Mile. City life looks as frenetic as it does today. Job mobility was unheard of in the Victorian office. Only by staying with the same employer was there any hope of security and a modest pension. The best positions were with banks and insurance offices. Those keen to climb the career ladder avoided Law Chambers, which paid the meanest salaries.

QUEEN VICTORIA STREET
1897 L130055

ST PAUL'S FROM
CANNON STREET   1905 L130164

In the 1850s, Cheapside was one of the most fashionable shopping streets in London, with a 'mighty stream of traffic' flowing through from Oxford Street to Leadenhall and the City. Because of its prestigious reputation and close proximity to the Bank, city financiers clamoured to live here, and annual rents from a single house could reach the incredible sum of three hundred pounds.

CHEAPSIDE c1886 L130066

At the junction with Paternoster Row, Cheapside swings
from the north in an arc and heads east towards the Bank.
Paternoster Row, on the right, was once a fashionable
shopping street patronised by Pepys and his wife. Nicholson,
the haberdasher and milliner on the corner, has an impressive
new frontage constructed in 1900.

CHEAPSIDE
C1905 L130273

Mansion House, the lavish building on the left, has been the official residence of the Lord Mayor for two centuries. It was built by George Dance on the site of the old stocks market. It has been said to have the air of a Roman palazzo. The portico is reached by flights of stone steps from the pavement and, from under the fluted columns, city workers could watch the throng of traffic passing below.

MANSION HOUSE AND CHEAPSIDE 1890 L130209

Richard Jefferies described the scene in the 1880s: 'Like the spokes of a wheel converging, streams of human life flow into this agitated pool... Blue carts and yellow omnibuses, varnished carriages and brown vans, pale loads of yellow straw ... this is the vortex and whirlpool, the centre of human life today on the earth.'

THE BANK OF ENGLAND AND THE ROYAL EXCHANGE
1890 L130208

Opposite the Mansion House is the Bank of England, a single-storey monolithic edifice, designed in 1734 by George Sampson. Sir John Soane devised some alterations to the west elevation in 1788. In late Victorian times there were nine hundred employees with salaries ranging from £50 to £1,200. The total salary bill was £210,000 - the sum a single top manager might earn today!

THE BANK OF ENGLAND
1890 L130179

Omnibuses advertising Dunlop tyres enter Threadneedle Street. Here was the famous American Coffee House, where merchants with interests in the colonies met to discuss business. On the right is horse-drawn cart of the Royal Mail.

THREADNEEDLE STREET AND
THE ROYAL EXCHANGE C1910 L130193

THE ROYAL EXCHANGE

1886 L130012

THE MONUMENT
c1890 L130187

This photograph shows the Cannon Street end of King William Street, which heads south-east from the Mansion House towards London Bridge. This dignified thoroughfare was conceived in 1835, and was much admired for its spacious and airy atmosphere. On the left is the City Luncheon Bar, and in the foreground a fleet of carrier's carts owned by Henry Drapper.

KING WILLIAM STREET
1880 L130102

This old inn, just over the river from London Bridge, was called by Stow 'one of the fair inns' of Southwark. In 1720 it was described as 'well built, handsome, and enjoying a good trade'. In this view it looks a ramshackle establishment, with Chinese-style latticed balconies and shabby cellars. It had shut up shop by 1885.

THE KING'S HEAD,
BOROUGH HIGH STREET 1875 L130131

Tugs towing flat-bottomed barges are still plying the Thames in this 1950s scene. Seventy years before there was a timber quay under the walls of the Tower, with tall-masted sailing ships edging through the raised bascules of Tower Bridge. The river here was thick with islands of logs chained together, floating heavily in the shallows.

THE TOWER OF LONDON
c1950 L1305022

This ancient fortress has served as arsenal, prison and royal residence, and is comprised of an irregular mass of buildings erected at various periods down the centuries. It was begun by William Conqueror, and it is his keep, the White Tower, that still dominates the scene. The moat was drained in 1843 and sown with grasses and shrubs.

THE TOWER OF LONDON
c1890 L130172

This crowded region south of the river was once the heart of London cockney life. The Elephant and Castle, a great meeting place of thoroughfares, was termed a 'ganglion of roads' by Dickens in 'Bleak House'. The squat old inn that gave it its name dominates the scene, and is offering hot and cold joints, chops and steaks to diners.

THE ELEPHANT AND CASTLE
c1890 L130028

CRYSTAL PALACE
1900 L130147

This monumental glass pleasure dome was created in Hyde Park by Joseph Paxton for the Great Exhibition of 1851. 2,000 workers erected it at high speed, bolting and welding together 3,300 iron columns, 205 miles of sash-bars and 293,655 panes of glass! It was a temple to the triumphs of Victorian art and industry. After the Exhibition, it was moved to wooded parkland at Sydenham in south-east London.

Pleasure seekers make the most of the winter weather skating on one of the many lakes. The Crystal Palace became a paradise for Londoners keen to escape the dirt and the grime. At weekends they flocked to Sydenham in their thousands to enjoy the displays and exhibitions - Blondin once walked a high wire here and cooked an omelette seventy feet in the air!

CRYSTAL PALACE
c1890 L130059

This ornate pleasure craft looks perilously low in the water, but the throng of passengers seem quite oblivious of the rising water levels. Queen Victoria was a regular visitor to the Crystal Palace, and once encouraged the Shah of Persia to sample its delights. These pleasure grounds were an unparalleled symbol of the continuing glories and achievements of her reign.

CRYSTAL PALACE
1890 L130060

Jubilee day was the perfect occasion for royal pageantry. After a service at St Paul's, the ageing Queen was driven in her state coach past Parliament and across this crowded bridge, escorted by her loyal troops. The bridge is decked with garlands.

WESTMINSTER BRIDGE
1897 L130219

Crowds gather on the steps of Gilbert Scott's imposing Gothic-inspired memorial to the Queen's beloved husband, Albert. The Guards' bandsmen, resplendent in busbies and bright red uniforms, are waiting to begin their procession.

THE ALBERT MEMORIAL
1897 L130011

The royal coach heads out across the courtyard of the Palace bound for The Mall. A throng of carriages waits to join the procession across London. Queen Victoria wrote in her diary that it was 'a never-to-be-forgotten day... No one ever, I believe, has met with such an ovation as was given to me ... Every face seemed to be filled with real joy'.

BUCKINGHAM PALACE
THE DIAMOND JUBILEE 1897 L130157

*Queen Victoria smiles graciously at her subjects from beneath
a parasol. The team of horses bend under the weight of
shining brasses and decorative tackle. Behind the coach stand
a gathering of be-robed dignitaries of the Church.*

DIAMOND JUBILEE DAY
1897 L130158

The barrel organ always drew a huge crowd with its wheezy renderings of popular tunes. When a trio of frightened monkeys was introduced the attraction for children was irresistible. Here they crowd closely round while the monkeys, dressed in waistcoats are goaded reluctantly into performing their tricks.

THE ORGAN GRINDER
1895 L130109

THE BOARDMAN
1877 L130118

THE MATCH SELLER

1884 L130116

GINGER CAKE SELLER
1884 L130111

There were continual public fears about the purity of London's water supply. In early Victorian times water taken from the Thames at Chelsea was infected with the contents of the city's sewers and the drainings from its dunghills. There were terrible widespread cholera outbreaks in the 1840s and 50s. The water seller shown here would have had a regular pitch so that clients grew to trust the purity of his water.

THE WATER SELLER
c1890 L1302002

By the 1880s the shoeblack societies had four hundred boys on their books. A number were given cheap board and lodging. These shoeblacks were licensed to trade by the Metropolitan Police and carried on their business unhindered. There were, however, many unofficial operators, who 'infested the streets and annoyed the passenger'.

SHOEBLACKS
C1890 L130119

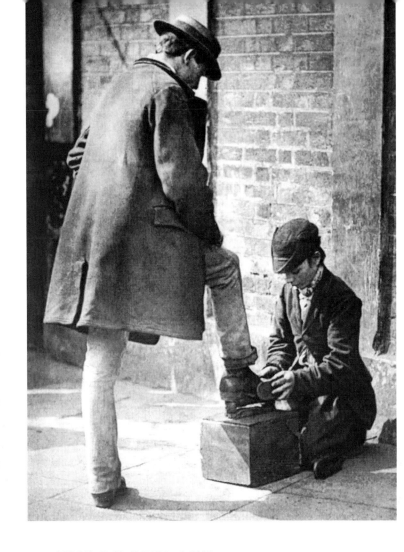

THE BOOTBLACK
1895 L130114

Bears had long been abused by Londoners. In the 17th century there was a popular bear garden at Bankside. This poor creature is urged to dance to bugle tunes played by his owner, who is probably an old soldier. Though tightly muzzled, this giant seven-foot bear must have terrified passers-by, as he complained at his miserable lot.

THE DANCING BEAR
1895 L130108

A bewildering number of morning and evening newspapers was available to the Victorian reading public, including The Daily Chronicle, The Times, The Evening News and The Morning Advertiser. In the 1880s and 90s, new printing technology released onto the market a wide range of cheap and tacky weekly magazines and comics. This old newspaper woman stands her ground under the spinning wheels of passing carriages.

THE NEWSPAPER SELLER
c1890 L1302004

This street trading woman is offering potatoes from her basket. Baked potatoes were even more popular with Londoners, and handcarts fitted with ovens and chimneys plied the streets offering inexpensive hot snacks. She looks relaxed enough but the weight of the potatoes must be excruciating.

THE POTATO SELLER
c1890 L1302001

Children cluster round licking at the cheap ice cream from the hokey pokey stall. They look like ragged street urchins in their rumpled suits and battered boots, and were probably bought their treats in return for posing for the photographer.

HOKEY POKEY STALL ,

GREENWICH 1884 L130110

This rather forlorn picture shows a tiny emaciated donkey pulling a cart selling strawberries. We associate this exotic and scarce fruit with jollity and celebration, but this trader and her son radiate only a sense of misery and poverty.

THE STRAWBERRY SELLER
1885 L130213

THE KNIFE SHARPENER,

WHITECHAPEL ROAD 1885 L130214

NOMADS

1885 L130212

INDEX

PLEASE HELP US BRING FRITH'S PHOTOGRAPHS TO LIFE

Our authors do their best to recount the history of the places they write about. They give insights into how particular towns and villages developed, they describe the architecture of streets and buildings, and they discuss the lives of famous people who lived there. But however knowledgeable our authors are, the story they tell is necessarily incomplete.

Frith's photographs are so much more than plain historical documents. They are living proofs of the flow of human life down the generations. They show real people at real moments in history; and each of those people is the son or daughter of someone, the brother or sister, aunt or uncle, grandfather or grandmother of someone else. All of them lived, worked and played in the streets depicted in Frith's photographs.

We would be grateful if you would tell us about the many places shown in our photographs—the streets with their buildings, shops, businesses and industries. Describe your own memories of life in those streets: what it was like growing up there, who ran the local shop and what shopping was like years ago; if your workplace is shown tell us about your working day and what the building is used for now. With your help more and more Frith photographs can be brought to life, and vital memories preserved for posterity.

We will gradually add your comments and stories to the archive for the benefit of historians of the future. Wherever possible, we will try to include some of your comments in future editions of our books. Moreover, if you spot errors in dates, titles or other facts, please let us know, because our archive records are not always completely accurate—they rely on 150 years of human endeavour and hand-compiled records.

So please write, fax or email us with your stories and memories. Thank you!

CHOOSE ANY PHOTOGRAPH FROM THIS BOOK

for your FREE Mounted Print. Order further prints at half price

Fill in and cut out the voucher on the next page and return it with your remittance for £2.50 for postage, packing and handling to UK addresses (US $5.00 for USA and Canada). For all other overseas addresses include £5.00 post and handling.
Choose any photograph included in this book. Make sure you quote its unique reference number eg. 42365 (it is mentioned after the photograph date. 1890 / 42365). Your SEPIA print will be approx 12" x 8" and mounted in a cream mount with a burgundy rule line (overall size 14" x 11").

Mounted Print
Overall size 14 x 11 inches

Order additional Mounted Prints at HALF PRICE - If you would like to order more Frith prints from this book, possibly as gifts for friends and family, you can buy them at half price (with no extra postage and handling costs) - only £7.49 each (UK orders), US $14.99 each (USA and Canada).

---

* IMPORTANT!

These special prices are only available if you order at the same time as you order your free mounted print. You must use the ORIGINAL VOUCHER on the facing page (no copies permitted). We can only despatch to one address.

Have your Mounted Prints framed (UK orders only) - For an extra £14.95 per print you can have your mounted print(s) framed in an elegant polished wood and gilt moulding, overall size 16" x 13" (no additional postage).

FRITH PRODUCTS AND SERVICES

All Frith photographs are available for you to buy as framed or mounted prints. From time to time, other illustrated items such as Address Books, Calendars, Table Mats are also available. Already, almost 50,000 Frith archive photographs can be viewed and purchased on the internet through the Frith website.

For more detailed information on Frith companies and products, visit

www.francisfrith.co.uk

For further information, trade, or author enquiries, contact:

The Francis Frith Collection, Frith's Barn, Teffont, Salisbury SP3 5QP
Tel: +44 (0) 1722 716 376 Fax: +44 (0) 1722 716 881 Email: sales@francisfrith.co.uk

Voucher

for FREE and Reduced Price Frith Prints

Do not photocopy this voucher. Only the original is valid, so please fill it in, cut it out and return it to us with your order.

	Picture ref no	Page number	Qty	Mounted @ £7.49 UK @$14.99 US	Framed + £14.95 (UK only)	US orders Total $	UK orders Total £
1			1	**Free of charge*** £		$	£
2				£7.49 ($14.99)	£	$	£
3				£7.49 ($14.99)	£	$	£
4				£7.49 ($14.99)	£	$	£
5				£7.49 ($14.99)	£	$	£
6				£7.49 ($14.99)	£	$	£

Please allow 28 days for delivery

	* Post & handling	$5.00	£2.50
	Total Order Cost	**US $**	**£**

Title of this book . . . .

I enclose a cheque / postal order (UK) for £ . . . . $ . . . .
payable to 'Francis Frith Collection' (USA orders 'Frith USA Inc')

OR debit my Mastercard / Visa / Switch (UK) / Amex card / Discover (USA)
(credit cards only on non UK and US orders), card details below

Card Number

Issue No (Switch only)   Valid from (Amex/Switch)

Expires   Signature

Name Mr/Mrs/Ms . . . .

Address . . . .

. . . .

. . . .

Postcode/Zip. . . . . Country . . . .

Daytime Tel No . . . .   Valid to 31/12/06

PAYMENT CURRENCY: We only accept payment in £ Sterling or US $. If you are ordering **from any other country, please pay by credit card**, and you will be charged in one of these currencies.